Printed in the United States of America

First Printing, 2015

ISBN : 978-0-692-58118-6

www.Amazon.com

Thank you

Thank you to everyone who supports me and my writing. It means a lot. I hope you enjoy this anthology of poetry as much as the first. Special thank you to Team Ayce for reading some of these and helping me edit them. I'm the beat and you are the tempo. I couldn't do it without you guys. Thank you so much.

Special thanks to my sister Chey, it is because of you I remain strong. Thank you for being a friend and the best sister one could ever ask for. I love you more than I could ever express in my words.

Ayce

As these words drip

Silently these words sit

Patiently in my fingertips

Till this emotion starts to slip

That's when the pain effortlessly drips

Through an inked tip

I write these verses like a script

The words are my bullets from a clip

Then I start to trip

Building up the bricks

No one can decrypt

What sits silently on my lips

I keep a firm grip

On my shoulder with the chip

In your face I will spit

As these words drip

From my fingertips

Anxiously I wait for the hit

To release all this bullshit

Kisses from the rain

If there was a chance tonight
That I could see you from the heavens light
You wouldn't have to ask me twice
To pay any price
We are forever connected
Your memory will never be neglected
When my life is the most hectic
You come to me as my medic
I look to this reddish orange sky
As I swore I heard you whisper Hi
No tears I need to cry
Because I know there is no goodbye
One day we will resume
Till then, I will keep these flowers in bloom
You make this white light shine here from the moon
So I kiss this stone as I whisper I'll see you soon
Knowing you are freed from your pain
From life's pressures that made you feel constrained
Even though, you had no time to explain
In my heart I know I can sustain
I miss you so much, but you I would never blame
It's just I long for your love from back in the day
There are so many things I still want to say
That's when your kisses ease me, in the form of rain

Dedicated to: Weeny

Rid of me (without fault)

This is my definition
Of this fucking depression
It's more than just a pain in your chest when you're stressing
Bigger than a lump in your throat when it's the truth you're digesting
You try to hide the pain so no one asks questions
You wouldn't understand unless you are in this position
The thinner my patience is stretching
The farther back I'm setting
Giving in, it isn't letting
It's going to be a long night, I'm betting
You think I'm saying it for attention
Then it's me you are not getting
When you choose to have loneliness as your only friend
Because you're afraid others will not comprehend
Why these wounds you can't fucking mend
If I could just break free from the grip of desolation
I wouldn't have to await demise with anticipation
Everything here causes aggravation
When a panic attack
Hits you like that
These fucking monkeys jumping on my back
The only weapon I have is a gat
I keep trying to pick myself up
But my brain is like what the fuck
The door with the light on is locked shut
I'm bleeding out from all these cuts
I just have had enough
Going through years of this shit has made me tough
Now my edges are rough
I want to smile honestly but no luck
I'm writing so I'm venting
But sometimes it's not enough then my vision starts fading
My head starts caving
Is my sanity really worth saving?
When it's soiled in hating
Relief is what I'm craving
These dark clouds silently roll in
Like a well-trained assassin
They can smell the sin

That I am drench in within
On the outside I'm trying to remain calm
While in the inside there is a fucking war going on
The sweat drips from my palms
This feeling is too wrong
When this pain stains my eyes
It makes me blind
To the sunshine
I'm trying so hard to clear the mind
But the demons keep pushing me back to the demise
Forcing me to remise
Dragging me to start back at square one
I swear they do it for fun
Till I've come
Completely undone
Nowhere left to run
I scream "Where the fuck is my gun!"
On my good days, they sit in the corner of my mind
Waiting for just one small trigger to make things decline
Rejoice, is something that is immediately declined
Depression once again becomes the mastermind

21

My little princess how you grew up to be
The most beautiful of all the queens
Just yesterday you were so little it seems
But time flew so fast right by me
To the first steps you took
To the first meal you over cooked
Or when I reminisce while I take a look
Through all your old yearbooks
These twenty one years of your life
Made me so happy to be alive
To me you have brought so much blithe
I wouldn't trade it for any price
Those beautiful eyes of blue
Glisten like the early morning dew
That makes me realize, there is nothing I wouldn't do
To bring out that big smile in you
Just know I will always be here
Whether you need a listening ear
Or to scare someone off with trembling fear
Know to you, I will always adhere
When someone causes you dismay
Don't worry, they have become my prey
I love you more than words can ever say
A love that will grow each and every day
If you feel you have lost your way
Take my hand it will be okay
Because you are strong and brave
I will protect you the best I can every day

Dedicated to: My little sister

Apple of your eye

This apple was shinny till you dropped it in dirt
Dulled from all the times I was put last instead of first
Something heartless in me you have unearthed
When our loving words abruptly turn into a sturt
When with others you carelessly flirt
I try so hard to just avert
These hugs goodbye do more than hurt
No longer am I your sun, your earth
Jealous by the way you say their names
The tone just isn't the same
Something about them keeps me out of the frame
Even though all of a sudden you started acting strange
I'm over reacting is what you claim
So inside, I burst into flames
Your sinful pleasures will catch up to you
When your lies become so transparent everyone will see through
In that moment you won't be able to do me like you do
Go ahead and curse me as the shrew
And you will forever be my rue
But know, only once will I play your fool

Her

She wanted me as her only lover
All the others
She wouldn't even bother
Because I make it so much hotter
She wants to make them play boys sour
As I'm making her scream louder
I love when she uses her power
To make me fall on her like powder
She said fuck the disclosure
As she pulled me closer
Do me how I want, slower
We tore it up like dozers
You cross those tan legs
Girl you know that makes me beg
In this intimacy we are so engaged
I could do this all night and day
I want all of you tonight
Don't turn off the lights
I need to look into those beautiful blue eyes of delight
And watch my emptiness take flight
With you it feels so right
Take me now she seductively replied

Church

You say I need Christ
To be in my life
To rid me of this blood of ice
That I will not suffice
If I cannot find the missing slice
Of my heart that is diced
From the ashes it will rise
To show my never ending sacrifice
To which I have survived
To this mind that is imprecise
I choose to live with this depression
Because I refuse to take medication
This pain has my dedication
The devil looks at me with admiration
Days that I say I want to be alone I mean it
I don't want to infect others with this negativity shit
Trying not to do myself in like the others did
So I stay soiled in this crib
Thoughts absorb the darkness
But I remain dauntless
Wandering eyes seem harmless
Till actions show the harshness

First Time

There was just something in the way
How you would slowly cross your legs
Those freshly painted nails grasped your chest
As you played with your necklace
When you would take a deep breath
Puffing out your breasts
Soothing it was as you read words
An angel's song is heard
How that tight black skirt
Showed off every voluptuous curve
The green color of your iris
Left my ruined mind tireless
Sweeping your black hair behind your ear
When I needed you most you would adhere

Green eyed monster

I have this crush I confess
The way you look right past me I knew you were dangerous
You're so damn gorgeous
But it's also so torturous
I could tell from your sashay
You would cause so much dismay
If you were mine, it's me you would betray
It would just end us that way
You are such a distraction
I try so hard to hide my reaction
But this emotion gets so much traction
Off your seductive attraction
The echo of your voice
Keeps my clothes moist
Leaving me with no choice
To have this emotionless poise
You make my heart skip a beat
But I make you want to be far away from me
I hate that you make my knees weak
Effortlessly these strings you suddenly tweak
If you gave me a chance I would sweep
You right off your tired feet
But I feel the constant defeat
With my persistent creepy keek
Your secret is deep within your cheeks
As your smile, slowly it leaks
Your exterior is angelic as can be
You could be my beauty and I'll be your beast
But I know buried inside you deep
Is an evil itching to be seen
Reality sets in when it's me you demean
But my thoughts remain so obscene
The more I observe the more I glean
You, the monster with eyes of green

This won't be pretty

I put this cold metal to my head
I think of all the things they have said
That make me wish I were dead
With these dirty sheets I make my bed
I don't want to see your fucking face
But we are forced in the same place
I want to spit on you, you disgrace
This is regret based
I've tried to convince myself we weren't real love
But you have done such a swell job of covering us up
Like what the fuck
I never mistreated you once
When these feelings hit
I tell myself I'm stronger than this
I don't need your fucking bullshit
Trying to keep this wound stitched
But you walked back in like a bitch
After a run of 14 months
You pulled some ridiculous stunt
You let me go like a cunt
Putting on some front
We were so good a month before
You threw my heart on the floor
You don't give a fuck that I'm sore
I know you feel nothing for me no more
So when our company is forced
Just do like usual, pretend I don't exist anymore

Silk Sheets

Silk sheets
Pounding heartbeats
I can feel the heat
When you're kissing me
As your hair gently falls
You whisper my name like a midnight call
Our shadows form one on the wall
My fingertips on your body crawl
This island breeze
Flies by so softly
Our I love you' comes so promptly
From your breath I get a whiff of your morning coffee
These moments I won't take for granted
I'll lay my kisses all over you like the sand did
You and I are off grid
So let's make the most of it
We are lost together in this stare
This warm embrace we share
Our time is limited it's not fair
But how deeply for you I care

If you only took the time

I always wanted you around
But in the bottle you chose to drown
How easy the 12 went down
Ignored me without a sound
Telling me to go play
Cuz the lotto was more your forte
Around others you would portray
A "perfect relationship" they would say
When your tilting hands become still
You will pick this book up and feel
The distress you cause me still
Know that after it all, myself I will heal
I try so hard to sift through my memory
But I can't remember many
Where it was just you and me
That's because there isn't any
I tried to forgive you for what you have done
I know it's not just you it's also the mom
If I had to pick who did more harm
The race you both have won
When I would wait for you for hours
You couldn't call to tell me why, you coward
The life in me kept going downward
Like the autumn does to a flower
When you finally realize these moments you cannot pull back
Love from me you will always lack
These pained memories will be all you have
They will forever remain in your tortured past

Autumn

The warm October breeze
Rushes through the tall grass weed
I hear the clanking of the flagpole chain in the distance
As the sun pushes through the clouds resistance
The needles fall from the pine
While the colorful leaves gently glide
Birds sing so loudly
While the kids across the street get rowdy
So silent this late Sunday afternoon
You feel the night coming too soon
Enjoy this glorious day till the last second
As a new day softly beckons

Cursed

I feel your claws inside
Your shadow by my side
Your rules I'm forced to abide
So for this I die
Hate is what I deify
Just to get me by
This is what it betides
The dark I confide
This depression is now verified
With the hurt you provide
Love you cannot ever requite
Your lips to me they satisfy
My love for you dissatisfies
I'm left to wonder why
Your wrongs you would never justify
I am far from being sanctified

As these years pass
Happy birthday my beautiful lil' princess
Holy jeez! You're 20! It's a bit hard to digest
You have always held that special place in my chest
Despite what you think of yourself, I think you are the best
I will always love you more than words can say
A love so strong it lingers till after my dying day
From the struggles, to the great memories we have
I would not take any of it back
We have and are in this together
As my sister and my daughter
To watch you grow into this beautiful woman you have become
Makes me beyond proud to be your sister mom
Big sis is going to be here for you always no matter what
If anyone fucks with you, I have my dukes up
Keep being the giggly, bubbly full of life gal alright?
Because you are a blessing for being the wonderful lil' bundle in my life.

Dedicated to: My little sister

Old friend

Hey there old friend
How the hell ya been
Is all well I been wonderin'
Or did you fade with the trends
Do I ever cross your mind?
Cuz you're always on mine
I've dialed your number a million times
But never pressed send I don't know why
Where did we derail?
When did our love become so frail?
We let distance prevail
The hurt was veiled
I always think what I would say
If we were ever again face to face
Would I just walk away?
Or your hands would I'd take
No need
For apologies
Just hope you see
I didn't mean
To just up and leave
So if you are out there
Know that I will always care
Never will I feel despair
What we had, nothing can compare

Could you be?

I saw the headlights pull into the drive
Should I run to you or go hide
I just couldn't decide
I began to see the beginning in my mind
From those gorgeous bright eyes
To your flawless laugh lines
If I put that all aside
Would I still make you mine?
Truth is I want you by my side
I miss you so much I cannot deny
I don't want you to hurt me another time
But I can't get you off my mind
Please tell me loving you is a crime
Or let's pick up where we left off and live our life
Please stop telling jokes
I'm trying to pretend this is a hoax
Forget all the love notes
I do not need this hope
So while you're holding me in your embrace
Swear you will take me far from this place
And I'll promise not to make the same mistakes
Only good times we will retrace
You wear it on your face
That it's your breath I take
So could you be my shining star?
Or will you leave me in the dark
So take my hand and the past we will disregard
Or give me your number so I can just discard

Black veil beautiful

She had a crooked smile
That would drive you wild
But her brain is so vile
You'll be choking on your bile
She showed me pain like I have never known
I feel so alone
But I can't let go
She will not atone
Her demons always have the munchies
Their snack of choice is always me
I'm addicted to this vagary
If I could I'd hang her in effigy
I never knew evil
Could be so beautiful
In a black veil
As I suffocate in my travail
She made love defile
Turned my heart into an ash pile
So when she is cutting me down to size
No remedy will suffice
From the pain in her lies
And red in my eyes
When truth becomes unraveled
And words are less scrambled
I'll give her more than she can handle
Forcing her to fight this battle

Grin and bear

Buddy you and I working our hand to the bone
When this mundane movement becomes so old
So tired of doing what were are told
Carrying everyone's work load
As the phony dressed business man
Takes my money from my hard working hands
To spend on his high class vacation
I'm like well god damn
Can a cat catch a break?
Have a piece of the cake
I work so hard and all they do is take
Fake ass smile with a firm hand shake

Beast

I cannot get no fucking release
Raging inside is this beast
Its wrath is unleashed
My emotions it has seized
The sickness won't let me be
The ending I cannot see
All the doors are locked I need the key
A helping hand I desperately need
I'm forever praying on my knees
Because this feeling never leaves

As we slip away

We lived in separate worlds
Ever since I was a little girl
The more time that passed
The more I couldn't stand your ass
We live day to day
Without anything good to say
You are asking stupid shit more than enough
My fist wants to do more than just a touch
When these tempers flare
Everyone can feel the tension in the air
Behind my back at me you stare
The less my heart for you cares
Bumping into each other without an apology
Fuck off these words happen periodically
You feel this coming to an abrupt end
So you tighten this leash without a bend
Making sure you get it all in
As you see this face diminishin'

The wolf and the pig

You really think you cross her mind
When I'm between her thighs
Giving it to her all night
She comes to me when you guys fight
I make her feel right
Your little peanut keeps her nice and tight
How's it feel to have your woman loving a "dike?"
That bottom lip I make her bite
You know she doing it outta spite
Now you are in this plight
I keep your side of the bed warm
While it's her you try to reform
She has already transformed
I got that bitch to conform
She loves that taste
Of me below the waist
My sweat I keep laced
All over her fucking face
So when you are kissing her mouth
It's me you are getting a little ounce
I fucked her all over your house
And you thought she was a loyal spouse
Why you think she is never in the mood
To give it to you
I make her feel wanted when she nude
Take off them clothes slow as I denude
Then all night we screw
My words a far from prude
That's why she likes talking to me dude
You will realize she was fuckin me instead of you
And you thought she was in love with you
Who do you think she is running to!
That's why she comes to me to get it done
Naw bro I don't even need a strap on
I get her off with just the tip of my tongue
Her whole body is sprung
With just one lick
Your girl all over my metaphorical dick
Hey she can take her pick

But I guarantee it isn't going to be you slick

Soulless

Bitch you make me so sick I can't even eat
My mind is so stuck on this self-defeat
Why are you saying we can't be
When you're the one who pursued me
Yeah open your mouth insert both feet
This respect becomes obsolete
You've said false things to pacify
I know damn well there is no truth in your eyes
When you gave we the boot you didn't even cry
Not a single damn tear fell from your eye

Prayer

This is the prayer
I'm stripped to the bare
Show the tears is rare
So I ask it's me you spare
While I describe my hearts affair
It's scattered, I share
Come close if you dare
Make sure you are prepared
Hate is in the air
To love me with err
My love tends to flare
Then feels nothing but despair
I know it's me you will ensnare
After my heart you impair
Make me feel like I'm walking on air
When I'm actually dying in midair
As I parish in solitaire

The trouble is

While you stand in front of her confessin'
In your fantasies It's her you're undressin'
Her crush for you it lessens
Your words you start regrettin'
She was just trying to hook you I'm bettin'
Deep in your gut you feel it settin'
When you swore to your heart no one is getting'
This guard you put up, down you're lettin'
So you flirt with each other
You thought it was you she wanted to discover
For a split second she thought of you as a lover
And for that now you suffer
When you make a bold move
So she knows you are saying truths
When you are gone she thinks nothing of you
Stuck feeling these old blues
When you thought you were the one she wanted
The first conversation haunted
This itch of wanting more vigorously taunted
False signals is what she flaunted
Thinking the both of you had that chemistry
She looked at you with such intensity
Thinking she would be your serenity
Because of her lenity
Now she has you so twisted
That temptation you wish you resisted
For it to go on you permitted
Her innocent words become so vindictive
Now you're forced to live with this embarrassment
Drenched with discouragement
That strong hug something you thought it meant
Till you die over her, you are fucking bent

Play it cool
My face became flush with that crimson color
As I spoke the words I want to be your lover
These feelings I desperately tried to cover
So the more they wanted to be discovered
I knew you didn't like me in the same way
But I continued to puke these words anyway
Just know you are as beautiful as a summer's day
I mean these words I say
Please don't laugh in my face
I'm just letting you know okay
I'm sure someone like you is used to the same
But I'm not like the others I'm not playing a game
I'm trying hard to play it cool
But I want you to know I'm so into you

Do me like you do

Lips so soft
Like a microfiber cloth
All over me you print that gloss
Command me, I know you are the boss
You kicked off those high heel shoes
Motioned me over to you
That was my cue
It was me, you wanted to pursue
I'm going to smear that blush on your cheeks
While we sliding on that minx
Baby if you like it kink
I'll have you at the brink
You won't have time to think
Into euphoria we sink
Touch me here
I'll kiss you there
Undressing me with that heavy stare
Girl when you do me like that, I don't even care
So much love I want to share
Run my fingers through your hair
Whisper in my ear what the fuck are you waiting for
Make my body sore
Have me screaming for more
Break this bed till it's in prices on the floor
I felt your passion saturate my core
That love I quickly absorbed
So babe now can you feel my heart beat
Take my hand let's see where it leads
I'll guaranteed to sweep you off of your feet
With you I want to make a mess of these sheets

Ruin me

When I'm left with the four corners of this room
And you leave the reminisces of your sweet perfume
This sunlight seems to become so gloom
I watch these roses die while in bloom
This is where I start dying
But I'm still trying
Through the tears I'm crying
I can feel the claws on my heart heavily sliding
My demons seize this opportunity
When we encounter this disunity
Your sickness I thought I had immunity
The thought of your face still ruins me
I just can't seem to quench this thirst
Of the kiss that came first
Before you became the worst
It's like you left a never ending curse
The sarcasm that I mistake for love
Hit hard like a bully with a shove
You made things unnecessarily tough
To the point where I have had enough

My own prison

With this dissension
Comes the depression
Then follows the regression
That leads to oppression
This feeling has become the obsession
For it to hold me as a possession
No more learning the lessons
Just only for the manic sessions
As you pray to your god in the heavens
The cries of demons beckon
As you count on your good reckon
Madness has adhered to my repression

Ms. S

Dear Ms. S
You were my first goddess
By far the best
Your time to me you would invest
To make sure I had success
I been crushin' on you I confess
It's my full attention you posses
My feelings I wish I could profess
But at the time I didn't understand
My yearnings as they would command
I would tremble from the soft touch of your hand
Unfortunate that my childhood was damned
I found an angel in you
It was all impromptu
These feelings were all new
I had no idea what love could do
What was this I was feeling
You just always looked so appealing
You made me want to climb the damn walls to the
ceiling
My heart beat was constantly speeding
To my eyes you were so pleasing
Your voice made me sweat when you were reading
The way you scratched your chest and crossed your
legs
Had me feeling some type of way
How those beautiful green eyes would convey
Taking me to a place
That was so safe
I purposely got detained
So with you I would remain
It probably sounds a bit insane
But it was with your time I wanted to retain
Even though I was so young
You were my first number one
Memories of you have clung
Years after your name has left my tongue

Low and behold

Low and behold
I'm trying to grow
I'm standing at this fork in the road
Which way should I go
How many times I've traveled these avenues
To make it half way and change my views
The bad decisions I choose
Direction is what I lose
I have paid my dues
But this darkness still chews

The golden side of the leaf

It's like these words were carved out of my heart
My blood is the ink in this pen making this art
I won't go outta my way
To ruin your day
But if the opportunity presents itself
Best believe you better check yourself
If I'm going down
You won't see me frown
I'll hold my head high and proud
Keep ahold of my crown
Because the strong woman in me is so profound
I'm no longer your fucking clown
I don't have it all
I never want it all
When times get tough I'll remain tall
No bitch you will not force me to crawl
As I'm slowly learning to forget
All my years my mind was someone's pet
I will succeed in efforts to retrain
And put more education in this brain
Build myself into the woman I want to be
I helped myself clearly see
That I really do have it in me
Regain my self-worth and esteem
The time is now to mature I highly deem
I took the wrong paths years before it seems
Turning over this new leaf
I never felt such relief
A goal that was hard to achieve
All I had to do was believe
So when you look into these blueish eyes of green
You will see a brand new me
There is a fire inside
I will not let it die
No matter how many tears I cry
I'm a fighter, I will survive
Things were a hurdle for me
But I was blessed to have this serendipity

The weight of depression

I've become unhinged
As these menacing thoughts infringe
On my mind as I binge
On the failure which is
For many years I have tried
Desperately to fix these broken pieces inside
Seems the more I did the more I died
So the less I would try
If you knew what it was like to feel this tension
Or never wanting anyone's attention
You would know the length of this dissention
That thrives on oppression
I'm trying to keep my mind clean
But this depression is so mean
The harder I would push the more it would demean
So I back down as if it were routine
When my brain takes a break
That's when it floods back in through the gates
These voices begin to berate
Just let me be for Christ sake
It gets harder every time
To flush this shit out my mind
I just can't get a grip on the whys
That I'm not healing with time
These demons surround me as I try not to blink
The pits of hell are closer to me than I may think
The ground around me starts to sink
Soon I will be extinct
The devil feeds me poison to kill me slowly
These demons will leave me lost and lonely
The monsters eat me alive till I am unholy
As I cower in darkness remorsefully

Under your skin
I'm about to crawl under your skin
Put my lips on your neck breathe you in
Lick that sweat off your chin
I know you are feeling it within
Trace my fingers where do I begin
Say my name girl with the Lynn
As we committing this sin
Got those toes on that cringe
Have you gone girl off the hinge
We waking up this whole inn
And you're making me melt with that grin
You want it all girl just say when
Damn them baby blues
I'm so lost in you
You are my muse
In writing this view
We won't stop there
You are telling me to come here
Put your fingers through my hair
I'll give you that loving stare
You can get me off
Just by acting tough
I know you like it rough
And you love how on you I crush
From that skirt huggin' your legs
To you leaning in that doorway
Your seductive foreplay
Has this cat feeling some type of way
Saying you could never let me go
I respond with these X O's
Ripping off them panty hoes
Your cheeks get that rosy glow
When you're calling the shots
That's when you're making it hot
No girl don't stop
Your turn to get on top

Something special

Smiling at me sitting on your leg
I remember those days
But has the alcohol made it a haze
You thought your memories were a phase
Now it's my company you crave
Any ounce of love I tried to save
But it turned to this hate
After it was me you betrayed
Childhood memories of you to rest I laid
I want nothing to do with you now I'm afraid
Father you could never wear that name
In these moments, your old age
Has made you ashamed
In these empty years I have sustained
I've become numb to your pain
Our picture is no longer in a frame
My young tears fell like rain
And you were the one to blame
So please don't make our visits constrained
I'm grown now and to this it came
This vacancy for you forever is ingrained

Tangled up

The feelings left me torn
The pain left me wanting more
It was you I once endlessly adored
Now I think of you as the dirty whore
The blood in my mouth I still vigorously taste
From all the words I should have not let silently waste
This shit makes me so crazed
I hate feeling this way
We were from two different sides of the track
A love that was bound not to last
I wish I knew the underlining lies that were facts
My heart I gave to you, I would quickly take back.
I just wanted to mean something to you
The way the fellas always seem to do
Now I know the truth
Those bitches are the proof
You swore it was my heart you would enshrine
I gave my all but you quickly declined
I love too hard with this heavy heart of mine
Now I suffocate inside cloud nine

The finest

Let's state the facts
You are nothing but a rat
Once you cross me there is no turning back
When I get silent that's when I attack
That's why they call me the sniper
I'll keep you shittin' your pants you are gonna need a diaper
Time to pay the piper
This shit gets me so hyper
Bet you didn't know your girl loves Chanel
This is where your anger propels
I am the rebel
I am as beautiful as a sea shell
And you're shit definitely smells
You put me through hell
But now I'm doing well
Seems like forever these wounds I would nurse
Getting through the winter months was the worst
I'm finally relieved from this curse
I'll let it all out from this pen as I disperse

Takes me back

Already gone
Was the song
You put on
When you said so long
I'll admit I forgave
But I won't forget the pain
I'm glad I didn't make you stay
I wouldn't make a good slave
Even though my all to you I gave
It was your black heart I could not save
If you ever wonder if I think of you
The answer is yes it's true
But don't worry It doesn't make me blue
And no it doesn't make us cool
You were right I always deserved better
For you I was a bar setter
I just couldn't accept our never
But the ties I had to sever
You would destroy everything I am
You were the Mary and I was the lamb
With you I wanted to start a fam
But you couldn't have gave a damn
Our fire started hot & red
Back when I believed the words you said
Who knew to this it led
As we burned out and became dead
I stopped fighting the inevitable
My love for you was irrevocable
But your love was inexplicable
Making me feel despicable
All the times
I sat up all night and cried
The feelings you gave made me I wanted to die
Because of your senseless lies
I thought for sure I would meet my demise
But as you know from the ashes I rise

Sugar to shit

We lost our magic
Our love became so tragic
You're not the person you want to be
That's something you always fail to see
Now you are my enemy
Say goodbye to our memories
You used to mean the world to me
More than you care to set free
But baby it's okay
You want to fucking play
With the hurtful things you say
That kept pushing me farther away
I tried so hard to keep my emotions at bay
But you force me to take more than I can take
Stop acting like everything is cool
You know I can no longer stand you
I'm done being the fool
You snooze you lose

Skitzo

I want to be with you no more I fear,
Never mind, don't come near,
You're coming home and I can't wait for you to get here,
I'm too scared to love you. You hear?
You make me happy and that's a fact,
But do I love you? Well I don't know about that.
I'm in love with you that's no lie,
I don't know so I'm going to let love die.
I want you to stay by my side,
I can't wait till we say goodbye.
All I want to do is spend time with you
I'll probably never date you.
Went from hugs I'm not ready to let go,
To one armed hugs just go.
Used to be good morning sunshine,
Now it's not good of any kind.
So I will say this in closing,
You I am disowning.
You will reap what you sow
Your favorite words will always be I don't know.

Missing you

I visit this stone frequently
As I'm missing you terribly
If you could only see
How much I love you weeny
I lay these flowers here
To let you know I still care
Even after all these years
This wound still tears
Sometimes the pain is still hard to bear
When I think of times we used to share
But I know you are finally at rest
You still hold a special part in my chest
Your reasons now I get
It makes me be my best
So I place this tender kiss on your stone
As I am reminded I will never walk alone
For it is you by my side you have shown
With me you will always be at home

Dedicated to: Weeny

As it fades

I love you more than my words will ever describe
No words from my mouth will be a lie
Only tears of happiness will fall from your eyes
This love of ours I cannot deny
Until I met you, I was just living life to get by
But you pointed me in a better direction with my life
One day I hope you want to be my wife
We will take the world on just you and I
This bond we share is more than love
It's like it's heaven sent from above
My heart fits in your hand like a glove
You are my lil' turtle dove
I don't want to live my life without you in it
Not even for a little bit
Right next to me is where you belong
Baby girl you know I'm not wrong
We are the perfect love song
My love for you goes infinity and beyond.
You do not have to say a thing
Your eyes tell me everything
I know you're lost in this moment with me
If only through my eyes you could see
Every ounce of pain
That was left in my veins
With one touch you drain
Then the bad just fades
Watch my heart unfold
Like the petals from a rose
You whisper, my heartbeat goes
I've suddenly forgotten all my woes
These dimples in your cheeks show
How something beautiful comes after the lows

Apathy

I feel the cold
I try to remain bold
Your words scold
Dwelling on how you made him a cuckold
It needs to be told
Cuz this shit is getting old
What you want is so jumbled
My world feels the rumble
Your love is so fabled
You think you are laying it all on the table
Your perfection of lies cover every angle
Making me feel so strangled
My heart you effortlessly mangled
As these webs you weave become so tangled

Again

I've exposed my pain
And all you can say
You do not feel the same
Why couldn't you tell me that yesterday
I'm sitting alone on this bay
Feeling less than okay
This demon has returned I'm afraid
My edges are becoming harshly frayed
Feeling again like I cannot continue the damn day
These thoughts burst so array
You abandoned me like a stray
So when you see me today
Remember I have nothing left to say

Don't Blink

I'm going to flip this page
To back in the day
When outside we would play
Till the sun would fade
Things seemed so simple then
All our time we would spend
On each other we could depend
I truly had a friend
If I could go back
To the times that made us laugh
Like the time we flipped the cart off track
Or how we would always have a peperoni stack
Counting coins we had lying around
To go get snacks in town
Going to hang out at the playground
Or just loving the music's sound
It seems as if it was just hours ago
That we were singing karaoke like pros
And playing with G.I. Joes
Where the hell did the time go?
But that's the beauty of growing old
Memories are pages we will fold
So we can relive them when we feel cold
That we once had good times as told
If I had a second chance to relive those
I would not hesitate, no
Those memories are so distinct
I cherish them more now I think
If I would have known a moment soon becomes extinct
I would remind myself to never blink

Sweet wine kissin'

Girl is it the red you tippin'
As the day is slippin'
Cuz you no longer trippin'
Must be what you sippin'
Cuz it lingers on my lips n
I can't get enough of this sweet wine kissin'
Now you are so jacked
I wanna take you in the back
Give it to you like that
How twisted you get this cat

Is it me

I'm so tired of this damn mundane
I'm sick of living this day to day
I keep telling myself I'll change
But I seem to be cemented in my own ways
Trying to fix this broken link
As this ship quickly sinks
The end is closer than I think
Slipping so fast like I'm in an ice rink
These wheels are turning so quick in my head
I'm waiting for them to drive me off the edge
These feelings I freely sketch
Relief from the agony seems so far-fetched
I keep making the same mistakes
I let myself keep wasting away
And these thoughts of my own life I'd take
If it wasn't for the loved ones' sake
Sometimes I can't help but wonder
What if I didn't make these blunders
Then maybe my heart wouldn't have to feel the sunder
So I say the words I'm okay with a stutter
As I relive my darkest moments
I become my own opponent
I try to desperately disown it
I constantly beg for this atonement

Dukes up

In these final moments of despair
I feel my heart tear
Should I even care?
I can no longer bear
Times like this I wish I was spared
I've tried so hard I swear
Even though I was so scared
So I'm on my knees in prayer
Gasping on my last air
As I whisper this isn't fair
I am prepared
I can no longer be repaired
Demons be aware
I'm coming full force in this flare
This is the end I dare

Mr. Right

You threw your head back
Gave out a loud boisterous laugh
Grabbed his knee as I passed
I'm reminded that nice guys finish last
That flirtatious look in your eyes
As you tell him of past times
You always knew how to draw in the guys
Whether it was with your truths or lies
Flipped your hair to the side
So to the others you vie
What spell is he whispering in your ear?
I bet it's all the things a girl like you wants to hear
His life he makes seem perfect it appears
So it's more believable with all the beers
I sit in the corner day dreaming
That it's me you feindin'
I close my eyes as you lean in
For that kiss he is theivin'
I wish I made you feel
That sudden thrill
Makes your heart stand still
Gives your body cold chills
Would you look my way
If it was his money I made
Or wore those shoes of suede
Looking so cool with Dolce shades
As he takes your hand
In my mind I'm saying God damn
But I must understand
You always wanted a man
To come creep
Into your silk bed sheets
You just love to feel the heat
Next to you when you sleep
I really hope it was worth it
And I really hope when alone you sit
It's memories of me that drift
Like a romantic movie skit

Just a picture

As I stare at this memory
Vivid like yesterday is the imagery
It becomes part of my documentary
You were such a reverie
How did we get lost in this fragmentary?
I would have loved you for centuries
But you soiled me with treachery
How could you do this to me?
My love now has so much mixture
Frozen from your coldness that embitters
My finger burning to pull this trigger
Under your breath you fucking snicker
Handing me this pain to hinder
You were supposed to be all that glitters
But you just leave these painful splinters
My heart has parish to cinder
So when these memories start to flicker
I will set fire to these pictures

Devil

The devil whispered in my ear to say
That's not heaven calling your name
Why must I constantly pay
With this dissention and pain
For all my mistakes I take the blame
But somehow I still get played
Day by day
No it's not okay
My character starts to fade
Like Sunkist suede
Here I lay
In a soiled bed you made
My thoughts in they cave
My hot passion to nothing is shaved
My love is taint
At this point I cannot be saved
From the monster I cannot tame
So it continues to maim

If you're down

If you're down
Babe we can skip town
They will be looking all around
But we will be nowhere to be found
We Cali bound
No turning back now
This connection is so profound
And you look wonderful in that gown
These feelings I expound
I'm wearing my emotions loud
I'll keep you safe and sound
You wear that crown
You always can astound
We will write checks and the whole damn bank will bounce
Only if you're down

III

I just can't help but think what are the lies about
That keeps me in constant doubt
When telling each other how we feel is no longer allowed
We are followed by this dark cloud
This is where our ship is going down
Perishing in the flames to which we are bound
Withering away without a sound
I bet you can fucking feel me now
Not remembering where we been
As I pretend
How's that feel under your skin?
Now karma will begin
As you hold me in this captivity
You rape me of my dignity
I have had it with your malignity
I am tired of feeling this morbidity

Confessions of the hopeless romantic

I have a confession to make
I love you so much my heart aches
To have you to myself I'll do whatever it takes
And no babe this isn't fake
Being with you I'm more than alright
It's like I'm lost in a beautiful paradise
My soul is on fire
With this burning desire
My love for you will never tire
I only hope to take our love higher
I just want to feel the pounding of your heart beat
Next to me every night I want you to be
I know at times I push too hard
It's just because I want you so damn bad this I can't
disregard
I know you think I deserve much more
But you have given me more than I've had before
I know you do all for me that you can
To show me your love and you're my #1 fan
Your constant efforts do not go unnoticed
My eyes are on you I'm totally focused
You're my heavenly dream come true
Years ago I wish I found you
But our times is now and I'll do what I do
Show you the love you deserve and hopefully you will come
to
The realization that not only are you my someone
But we are each other's ONE
If I lost you I would lose my life, my everything
My love and devotion to you goes deeper than any ring
Through time I will show you these things
My love you are amazing
I want you by my side every step of the way
I love you more than anything that's what I got to say.

Not my bitch

When you come crawling back
That's when in your face I'll laugh
Saying he can't make you cum
He can't do these tricks with his tongue
I'm the one getting you sprung
I make the sex fun
You never wanted me to leave your bed
Saying I gave you the best head
I remember all you said
Like how you're tired of the men
You weren't concerned about your man last night
When you were kissing all on me an between my thighs
Telling me it felt so right
And I felt so good you wanted to cry
You used to love my stories
Now I'm just plain boring
I realized I'm just talking to myself
You're too consumed with yourself
I can't amuse you any longer
Guess I'll be on my way I'll get stronger
Don't think I'm going to come running
When I'm lonely and need the loving
I'm not the one to do the fronting
I remain straight stunning
If you are wondering why you're not in my phone anymore
It's because you're dead to me duh whore
If you just wanted some ass
You should have told me that before I got fucking attached
You were only good for a fuck
I wink and you give it up
I bet he didn't' know you are such a slut
You love it when I'm all up in that butt

Dis-Connect-Shun

One day I'm gonna snap
And you're the one in my path
So when that thunder claps
I'll hide these bloody palms in my lap
As I silently laugh
Because you underestimate my wrath
Told you don't push this cat
I will push back
You make me so fucking mad
Your bullshit, enough I've had
I'll suffocate you with this bag named glad
We are forced to live in the same shack
You are the one I want to attack
In a straight line you cannot keep the facts
If I were you I'd watch my back

The fool
Stop your lyin'
Quit your cryin'
I know you're hidin'
Shit I ain't buyin'
There is no denyin'
The shit I'm findin'
It just ain't slindin'
This cloud you ridin'
Inside I'm dyin'
So I stop tryin'
To you it looks satisfyin'
So I'm goodbyin'

When nothing is left

She threw her hands in the air
That's when I went for her fucking hair
We maul each other like grizzly bears
We felt the stitches start to tear
How quickly we seem not to care
So our connection continues to wear
Even though I love you forever, I swear
Hurt me she said she wouldn't dare
You used to be perfect
And I used to be worth it
Now we both the culprit
In this case of bullshit
Girl I'm always hurting
So this is where you're learning
My love is worth earning
And I always kept your heart burning
As you're falling deep into my ocean eyes
Your silence classifies
You are carelessly eating me alive
For reasons untold I'm chastised
I'm gasping for life in this selfish demise
The only one that will survive
Is your demons infected by lies
As they start to colonize
I stay lost in your eyes oh why
You're in this selfish disguise
That the darkness will abide
Discouragement waits to destroy me from inside
Our feelings stand still
So these wounds cannot heal
It's like we made hate a deal
If we move forward it will kill

Cling

I only get clingy
When I know you are lying to me
You know how to feed
This jealousy
I wear my heart on my sleeve
You think it's cool to deceive
You falsely make it up to me
So you can pretend it's all fine and dandy
I know I have a short fuse
My anger is my muse
I love hard
Even when my heart
Is black from the char
Gushing from this scar
We try to start with a clean slate
But that's when I make a mess of the plate
So I tell you to kick rocks
All you do is talk
Never do you walk
So give me back that jewelry box
Stop trying to apologize
The hurt is deep within our eyes
I can't forgive you for what you did yesterday
I can't just pretend everything is ok
You made me so perturbed
With this emotional rollercoaster
Made me feel like I had no worth
Words I would say where unheard
But if the situation was in reverse
You'd swear I was fucking her

Become third best

Don't get this shit twisted
This wasn't permitted
But your silence admitted
That you are totally convicted
Of being that vixen
Now I want you to listen
I'm very complacent
No I do not need a replacement
Stop being so persistent
Obviously I'm resistant
I can do with or without you
I'm alone and with that I'm cool
I see it in your eyes I'm no fool
To be your toy I refuse
Play the game with me and you will lose
Be careful which one of us you choose
If it isn't me I guarantee you'll sing the blues
Have you drowning yourself in that booze
Honestly put yourself in my shoes
If you had to compete
With another three
Would you let go so easily
See as I see

Damn you

You have me trippin' on how it used to be
Like from the beginning
When you were so into me
You just could not wait to see
My smile like it was a treat
In my car making that heat
Your toes curling on your feet
Staring at me from the passenger seat
Those honey eyes so sweet
The times you didn't want me to leave
Pulled me in begging me please
Girl with me I thought you were down
False assumption I found
You started hating on me without a sound
And I started thinking out loud
When it starts to show
After you lost that glow
Tie my tongue in that bow
While you are out being a ho
Those nights when I had you so anxious
Using that provocative language
Fucked me like there was so much anguish
I was no longer taintless
I thought we were cool
But you left me feeling blue
Who fucking knew?
I wasn't the one for you
Ventured on to someone new
So damn quick too

Froze

As I take this heavy breath
It lies deep within my chest
As I long for the success
I give my all, my best
What is it I stand for?
As I stand here before
I can feel the cold floor
Taunting me once more
They ask why is it I come
That's when the cat has my tongue
I feel the wheezing in my lungs
This agony once again has begun
When I become my most silent
This dark has become reliant
On the suns defiance
Inside I feel so violent

In the pit of the stomach

As this blood continues to run thin
These feelings are shown on the outside rather than within
As the pain harbors this hate begins
Forcing another fake ass grin
I never needed a drink or a drug
To get me through the rough
I let it all go with a shrug
As the inside self-destructs
When this depression tears you apart
You feel nothing in your heart
Tired of being pushed back to the start
So I remain tart
It gets so hard to find it in me to push through
I'm left looking like a fool
Because I can't keep my cool
Acting like it's me you knew
Now I have you fooled
This evil you have fueled
These days are so life less and dull
I crave not to feel at all
This darkness enthralls
My soul it silently calls
I wish I could break free
From all that has a hold of me
Pushing through all my debris
The sun I can only oversee
Under that gorgeous exterior
Lies something so inferior
It remains superior
I wish this was easier
In the pit of my gut
Here is where it deeply cuts
To you I don't mean much
What the fuck

Somethin' bout' you

My life is in disarray
But I think you want to take me away
Baby girl I can't stay
But I'm down to play
I don't want to get attached
And I don't want to keep taking you back
I don't want to hurt you that is a fact
I just want to be all up in your snatch
The way that you are folding that cloth
To that shinny lip gloss
I'm having these obscene thoughts
Of us in some abandon loft
Why am I feeling this feeling?
Something about you has me fiending
That smile girl is so appealing
In your eyes, it's your heart I'm stealing
If we were to take this further it would be forbidden
But honestly that was a given
I just don't want to be smitten
And I don't want to be your addiction
I cannot seem to rid you off my mind
Maybe it's because to me you are so kind
Or the way the light makes those big eyes shine
I just want to grab you from fucking behind
You are killing me
With those skin tight leggings
It's like you are fucking begging
For this sexing
We don't need this
To turn into something more than what it is
I just want to full fill your curious
But I don't want you to feel the guiltiness
Those green eyes have me melting away
Please tell me we have nothing left to say
So I can go on about my day
I don't want to miss you in this way

The embrace I yearn for

My demon I know
Why I cannot let you go
Even though
You bring me so much sorrow
Bringing no hope in tomorrow
And whatever else may follow
You hold me close when I am alone
When my sadness is something I cannot condone
I am one of the suffering you have clearly shown
Depression is what I hone
When the others have left me for dead
Your voice is the only one in my head
My pain is what you are fed
The bleeding words I forever said
This icy embrace you have me in
Feels like I've committed a million sins
The darkest corners I have been
When you are hurting it's me times ten
It's the happiness you will suspend
Forcing me to only you I will befriend

The power in your eyes

When you give me that I want you stare
My love inside I want to share
Being without you is hard to bear
When you squeeze after a long day I know how much you
care
I have no doubts about us
You are the one I know I can trust
Kissing you every night for bed is a must
When we make love it's deeper than just lust
I'll go and do whatever you want without a fuss
I find it so sexy when you cuss
I do not see living my life with no one but you
I love everything that you do
To every effort to every I love you
I'm falling more in love and I hope you are too.
When I day dream of years ahead
I see us laying and laughing in bed
I see you laying on my chest as I'm petting your head
I see me showing you how much I adore this life to which I
was led
I see me rubbing your body down after a hard day
Making you dinner and boiling water for your tea as you lay
One look at you and I know everything is okay

The thrasher

For you I'm too real,
I say words to kill
My style is totally ill,
Makes you want a pill
Yea bitch I'm hardcore,
I have a shutout score,
Still nursing from the knife wound in my back
Didn't think I'd say shit about that?
You put my heart through the ringer,
Your love is a poisonous stinger,
You made me feel so small you could
squish me between your fingers
The headache constantly lingers,
I'll call you out anywhere
Pass you by will be rare
Piss me off if you dare,
Don't be acting like you're scared.

So Dumb

Damn this fucking cupid
Had me acting so stupid
You did me so wrong
But I got to remain strong
I won't stand here waiting forever
Wondering when you're going to sever
Those ties with him
I'll hang myself from a fucking limb
Before I waste my life on you
I'm tired feeling this dark blue
Bitch don't get me twisted
It's you I resisted
You had my heart
From the very start
You know you want it
Why you acting like a shit
Saying you don't feel me like that no more
Girl I thought we were good but you are
rubbing this sore

Midnight blue

I can smell that intoxicating perfume
Like you just walked into my room
The setting instantly turns gloom
I don't know what to do
There was a time you brought me happiness
Now you just bring the loneliness
Your memory is an illness
That makes my heart have stillness
These feelings I have for you have many shades
I hope that one day
I can permanently get away
From this drawn out tragedy that you effortlessly display
Along with your kindness you falsely portray
I was your seven year itch
To repair your marriage
Took what I would give
To get your curious fix
Now you threw me to the ditch
Treated me like a bitch
Don't expect me to forget
How you chewed me up and spit
So keep in mind
While I pull out of this drive
I was the one that made you feel alive
And kept your ass 100% satisfied

Not the same

I sat with tears in my eyes
While you told me that cold goodbye
On an iced December night
But it's alright
I've grown tired of your selfish lies
I can't take another sleepless night
Girl if you got to go just go
Your heart is so cold
I let you go your separate way
I have nothing left to say
But things just are not the same
Since you have gone away
Your insincerity
Is really getting to me
Like how you can up and leave
Girl with such ease
To your friend's you would rave
Now days
You just wave
Girl don't act like we are okay
Things just are not the same

Afraid of the dark

These emotions are uncontrollable in the dark
So dead is my beating heart
Things that take me so high
Eventually let me sink till I'm terribly dissatisfied
I'm so run down
My feet are cemented to the ground
My demons won't give up till they seize
All that is left of me
Trying so hard to break free
I can't fucking breathe
I long for the silence
To which my depression is reliant
Happiness becomes defiant
The demons bask in the triumph
Pushing reality far away
To avoid this day to day
Of this tiring mundane
As I lie straight to your face
Saying I'm okay
Begging for a sunshine ray
I just want to be alone but never am
The devil made me her lamb
This hatred she forcefully crammed
Now I am forever damned

Assimilate

Trust me, I know what it's like
When pain lies down with you every night
Clenches your chest so tight
Tiring out the words "It's gonna be alright"
I know what it feels like to fucking burn
Bullshit I have been though, your stomach would turn
Forced to grow up at a very young age
A responsibility I could not disengage
Dealing with those who are emotionally vacant
Have love but then it's abruptly taken
Mother couldn't put down the bottle
And father couldn't give up the lotto
Those footsteps I never wanted to follow
Those things tend to leave us so hollow
After they are lost and swallowed
Then all that is left is your silent sorrows
So that's when I decided to make something of myself
Play my hand the best with which I was dealt
Here I am sitting in front of you
With nothing left to lose
I'll take the cheers along with the boos
I'll keep pushing through
Keeping my head up like I always do
Dealing with this nasty bruise
Moved out to do things on my own
Then fail miserably because I wanted to do it alone
Let me tell you, it's not cool to be an adult still living at
home
Constantly feeling like a fucking mome
I've watched someone I love kissing on someone else
Then have to sit in silence and keep the anger to myself
I been pushed around in this hell as a kid
Lived through shit I shouldn't have lived
Been blamed for others mistakes, cuz they can't mind there
biz
But I've accepted what is
Do not feel for me
I do not want anyone's' sympathy
I just want to help someone through when times get rough

I'm telling you, one persons' love can be enough
I have seen things that will have you shaken
Tell you things that will have your heart breaking
Brainwashed into thinking I'm always in the wrong
Walking these roads when they seem 1,000 miles long
Pushing through this blizzard with only holey jeans and a T-shirt on
Just because some bitch convinced them all you don't belong
3 a.m. fuckers knocking at my door, scared shitless
Because no one is around to be a witness
Falling asleep to the sound of gun shots
My ears ring from the loud ass pops
Fuckers hiding in my backyard from the cops
Across the street there is a few more drug drops
The smell of sulfur makes you want to sneeze
Burning in my nose is that stale ass weed
This fucking factory
Is fucking stressing me
Get a raise of a dime
How the hell am I to survive?
These lazy bitches making bank
Because they have a higher rank
While I bust my ass
For this monopoly cash
Only scars left from the wounds I nursed
The winter months were always the worse
There is sun after that rain
In life, this you will ascertain

Cold

The only thing I've learned from love
Was how to shade it in with a grudge
While it eats my heart like chocolate fudge
I'm drowning in my ice cold blood
This loaded gun lies silently under my bed
Awaiting my approval to kiss the side of my head
I'll throw our time into the flames
Yes I will take the blame
For us swerving out of lane
But know I always loved you without shame
They say there is something wrong with my brain
This hatred for love I gain
As this absence of emotion engraves
Deep into my veins
When these memories creep up from behind
You have to let them burn from inside
Those clouds are silver lined
With fibers that keep your heart in a bind

Just let me be

Just let me be
You're eating at me
You took me by my heart
And watched me fall apart
Years later I still fall short
This love life is so morphed
For it's the acceptance I've longed
I had to grasp I just do not belong
I force myself to go on
But I know I don't belong
My heart will heal and memories will fade
But it will never amount to what you gave away
Treated me like a fucking asset
I'm still gushing from this wound from your hatchet
If you only had a damn clue
What I been through
In this moment I should say something for us both
But I choose to keep my mouth closed
My words will end up being poorly chose
As this distance between us so far it goes

The Key

I found this key to open my disturbed mind
To let all this pain shine
When a broken heart and angry thoughts combine
It's far from any kind of Valentines
What the hell you know about grown up in a broken home
What the hell do you know about everything being taken that you own?
Fighting these endless battles alone
At a young age forced to be grown
These fucking bullies make a cat wanna die
But while you were spitting in my eye
I made these tight ass rhymes
You shook now and this is why
I made something outta myself now
Your jaw is on the ground
Like oh wow
Because these feelings I expound
I still have my pride and dignity
You can't take that away from me
Even when you spew all your malignity
Your words remain elementary
Your bitch ass is white as snow
Cuz I'm calling you out bro
You just couldn't let shit go
So I'm going to eat you alive on this flow
You can't fix a gushing wound
With a Q-tip and just assume
I'll forget the past
I'll light a fire under that ass

Old friend (Part two)

Hey there old friend
How the hell ya been
It's been so long since I don't know when
How's life, I've been wonderin'
Do I cross your mind every now and again?
Our days blew away with the wind
I miss the laughin'
Whatever happened?
When I think of you
It doesn't make me blue
It makes these memories feel new
Those feelings I will never lose
It makes me feel like I'm young
Like my youth had just begun
Loving it like the morning sun
In a field we freely run
Holding your hand just having fun
Promises of things we would overcome
Then I feel a gentle breeze
A soft rustle in the leaves
It's so quiet could this be
The end for you and me
I'm on my tired knees
Just begging please
I've thought about what I would do
If I were standing right in front of you
Would I think it was too good to be true?
Or confess I couldn't stand to lose
So here I am open hearted
Tell me we aren't the departed
Let's pick back up where we started
I'm so sick of being downhearted
We haven't seen each other in ages
We have gone through so many changes
Our lives have taken so many stages
I guess a goodbye is as hard as they say it is

Swim

My head is swimming
This life I'm not winning
Something has to give in
As I keep these faults hidden
I continue to still be sinning
My head is spinning
I can't stop where do I begin
This head of mine I'm swimming through
I'm drowning too
On thoughts of you
Leaving me with no clue
As to
Why you do me like you do
Questioning myself who I am, a fool
These things I knew
I should have used as tools
Instead of blues

Sanction of my demons

My conscious has all this vacancy
These memories dwell so painfully
Forcing me to speak so hatefully
Even though I tread so carefully
I'm biting down on my anger so hard
But this hate pushes me so far
Leaving hells door open ajar
Reminding me of the monsters we are
I can't show you this demon I have become
Just show you where it derives from
My heart feels so numb
I shall be treated like scum
You have no clue
What it is to feel as I do
Yes I will always blame you
Bitch you are so cruel
I won't force myself to be
This image of someone happy
I know that's how you in vision me
But I'm saying that's not thee
I couldn't fucking care less
Okay sure I'm a damsel in distress
Or better yet
I'm a junky for being depressed
When this monster is trying to attack
I'm warning you get back
Restraint now days is what I lack
I'm trying to avoid all contact

She wasn't worth it

When you effortlessly pass me by
This is when you start acting like
You don't know me right?
I can cut you out of my life
So do not think you're the only one who can be hard alright
This shit isn't easy
When you are being sleazy
Girl if you don't want me I'll get to skippin'
So when you see me with another don't be trippin'
You put your hand on my thigh
Told me you do not want this, but that's a lie
In my darkest moment you reappear
Leaving your nasty words to adhere
Your intentions are still unclear
The claws from your fingers continue to dig deeper
Your eyes I will forever fear
As I scream I do not want to be here
My cries you silence so no one can hear
Over my shoulder you constantly peer
You do not know what these eyes have seen
My sense for bullshit, yeah real keen
The shit you did to me I'll get you back
Cuz karma is going to hit you like a heart attack
Knock your stupid ass out flat
This bleeding heart has turned black
I used to love you more than anything that's a fact
Everything and anything you wanted I'd blow my stacks
And you still left my like that
You treated me like a lab rat
You shattered my heart like glass
Now I'm going to light a fire under that ass
Fucking dumb ass cocks behind my back
Oh you thought I knew nothing about that!?
Well it's really hard to look past
Your loose ass snatch
You will not fool this cat

These twisted little things

I met this fine fox in Texas
We were both getting over the Ex's
Her smile was so infectious
She was intriguing and dexterous
It started with a hair twirl
The scent of that vanilla Carmel swirl
When her hair was in curls
All I could say was damn girl
She made the winter months so bitter sweet
Of course she would make me feel more than the summer heat
This relationship was so innocent
We were drawn to each other in an instant
An interest in her I would implement
That's when I lost my vigilance
We could laugh about it all
Wasn't a problem we couldn't solve
Disputes were quickly resolved
My worries she absolved
Her company was so comforting
New feelings I was discovering
Who knew she was just the type of girl to get me suckering
The heartlessness in her, that smile was covering
The joy and pain that they bring
Damn these twisted little things
Her long brown hair laid on her back
Thought this woman was gonna give me a heart attack
Now and then at me a smile she would crack
Thought I was on the right track
A playful touch and smack
I knew I'd get her in the sack
But the way she nibbled on my heart like a snack
Fuck man how she could do me like that
We would fight about stupid shit
I've come close to giving her a violent hit
When she would lie to me I kept a closed fist
Kept me hanging on because she couldn't yet commit
She swore to others I wasn't her cup of tea
But that's not what I would see

So I became the absentee
That's when she finally latched on to me
The joy and pain that they bring
Damn these twisted little things
Those harmless little winks
Turned into me giving it to her on the kitchen sink
She used to love how I was distinct
And I used to love how she tasted after a drink
Saying where have I been
Like it was me heaven would send
Our time she wanted to extend
She wanted me more than a friend
Money on me she would spend
My name she would defend
But there was something inside of her I could not
comprehend
After everything she still wanted him
Could not stand being away from me
 She repeatedly tested my sensitivity
I took it with passivity
I was blind to her cold propensity
Suddenly she saying she needs her space
She is straight lying to my face
She found someone to replace
What I had deeply emplaced
Sorry I'm not a fuckin brainbox
Or an ignorant pretentious cock
Handing me back that jewelry box
She is swearing we are lost
Insincere was her goodbye
Didn't even shed a tear from an eye
Her love was awry
Love me forever was falsely implied
The joy and pain that they bring
Damn these twisted little things

You lost me

I lay my head on this cold cast iron sink
I just cannot figure out what to think
You took it all away like a rat fink
We were complete, now we have broken links
So I cry a little to let it out
Accept the fact of what you are about
Wipe away all the doubt
What you are, is now so announced
The more I cuss
The more you lust
Just let go, so I can rise above
Instead I push, so you shove
Then you put this fence between us
Ignoring me with your what's
I just cannot get enough
Just because I forgive you
Doesn't mean I forget the things you do
This deceit you pursue
Is something you cannot undo
We were one in the same
Your touch would aflame
For that you made me feel so strange
This hatred made us estranged
This life time of love I once had
Was changed for your constant bad
I felt like such a fad
Since you left me just like that
His lips must have tasted as good
As you made them fucking look
On me, you're no longer hooked
My whole damn world was shook
I'll build my strength through this pen
Your time to me you just lend
That moment you let go of my hand
I knew, this was just a means to an end

The struggle

I'm trying to paint this vivid description
When happiness is a failed prescription
How it feels when it sets in
As I start to feel it burnin'
I'm filled with so much emotion
When my pen hits the paper it's an explosion
This pain has caused this erosion
I'll be gone at 30 the rate I'm goin'
Is it my buttons you are pressin'
Why is it me you are testin'
I'm dying, I'm confessin'
This hurt never lessens
My mind just isn't restin'
How you feel, always keeps me guessin'
But you don't give a fuck, I'm bettin'
There is something I'm just not gettin'
Saying I'm the one with the obsession
But you're the one who needs possession
I'm in constant competition
So my love feels the regression
I just want some decompression
From this fucking depression
Now I'm standing in this kitchen
Knife to my throat I'm itchin'
Cuz you're always bitchin'
We are constantly tiffin'
Your heart I fill like rippin'
The alcohol you keep tippin'
Getting through the day is a mission
This is where I start trippin'
Are we even worth fixin'
I'm slippin' I'm slippin'
This life I'm not gettin'
Trying to get where I fit it
But the dark clouds my vison
I'm just a creep from where you're sittin'
But if it was my life you were livin'
Then you would see how I'm driven
If the words from this rhyme

Have you thinking I'm ass o nine
Then don't ask me if I'm fine
I'll let these words sink into your mind
Bitch I know you are creepin'
When I'm fuckin sleepin'
These secrets you are keepin'
Has my tears fucking seepin'
Waking up to the sound of gun shots
It's my fucking alarm clock
Trying to keep this anger on lock
But it's hard with the shit you concoct
Stuck in your box
Swallowing these damn rocks
You make me feel as useless as a butter knife
When in this life
I just cannot seem to get it fucking right
These hands are so bruised from all the strife
It's like you're a fucking statue
Your love has no value
Salty as a damn cashew
So short is your purview
Do I dare continue?
When all we do is argue
Every fucking day it's a struggle to keep my mind clear
Look out! My words are nuclear
And if you wanna know how I'm feeling it's insincere
So don't ask if you can help, it's gonna be something you
don't want to hear
You keep sending these emotional voided vibes
Your selfish demons are eating me alive
I feel there is nothing left inside
I just can't seem to keep you satisfied
Your tireless rules I can no longer abide
I'm so done with this hellish ride
That you keep me on, tight by your side
You keep telling me to pray
When you are the one that has confessions to make
These mind games I can't take
So inside, in pieces, I break
Putting my fucking life at stake

Please tell me I'm making a mistake